EUPHEMISMS

KEVIN STENDAHL

Contents

E

1.

There's a circle on the human face that exists
between the bottom of the eyes and the top of the
chin, from the edges of the lips that sit closest to the
ears, inwards.

A gravitational pull speaks with conviction
throughout this space and you are the sound of
falling. There is a center. There is a radius. There are
dimensions and there are measurements. It exists for
a purpose, and it forgets to be on time.

It is capable and perfect, bright and blooming with
color; it is simple and understood.

To watch this space move is to exist without a sense
of urgency or of time at all.

When science prays to this portion of nose and lips,
which define scent and taste with an illusive tongue,
she dashes through teeth carrying syllables less fit
for ears and more designed to keep gods interested
in cleaning out the gutters on a Sunday afternoon.

Science is a "She"

2.

I want to become fertilizer when I die.

While in a jail cell, I overheard a guard tell an inmate that if you stick a rose on a corpse, it doesn't make him talk, and this never made any sense until now. Maybe if I dress the part a funeral will follow, and when it gets here, I'll be prepared. While I'm waiting for everyone else to cry and eat egg salad on white bread, I'll walk outside and breathe deeply before resuming the day.

I'll draw a picture of a vessel and name it Michael and wonder if Michael is a male or female name. When Michael is complete, shoes tied and buttoned-up, I will ball him up and throw him on the floor next to the bin. The bin will say, *Hey pick that up*, so I'll kick the bin over and passionately set its contents ablaze. She will hate me and no one will lose sleep over it.

After all of this has happened, I'll mistake a

man for a trashcan, knock him over for telling me
what to do, and light him on fire.

This is when I'll be sent to kangaroo court and the
jury (filled with mostly men and women) will throw
tomatoes at my feet, and find me guilty of all
charges. I'll look at my lawyer, and she will tell me
that *this is just a strict county*, and that I should have
taken the offer. The offer would have been to plead
guilty to littering and damage of private property
and spend 6-9 months picking up trash on the side
of I-94 with a long and pointy needle.

I'll accept my punishment as I walk through a series
of hallways to my cell, where I'll put on big cement
colored clothes and brush my teeth more than I
would at home. I'll name all of my belongings
Rosie, and they will all have red hair and wear green
clothes, but they're very quiet and never speak to
anyone else but me.

Tumor

3.

Time inevitably sifts through the dull, irrelevant and superfluous moments.

Absence sits patiently waiting for substance; like Tolstoy panning for gold, or Hélène's abortifacient overdose.

By mathematics, dumb luck, or vacancy, my editor is an historian.

He advises me towards the removal of words like *superfluous*, *irrelevant* and *dull*, but no matter how many times Stalin told Ivanovov to stop fucking gorillas, no one was going to win a war by practicing artificial insemination.

The Greek

4.

In a stale apartment kitchen she stands behind a
man, sitting in a wooden chair, and lights a cigarette
while they watch their neighbor's house burn down
behind them but in front of them on the TV.
The girl with the cigarette says that *sometimes it's
right under your nose*, but she really means that *it's
better late than never* and they all wait for their turn
to be on the TV in the house across the street's
upstairs bedroom.

Television

5.

Life has been throwing itself at me lately. Nighttime argues with my mornings, and fuck, who knows what a throwaway life is, in comparison. In both and either option, the wind is still blowing rain towards, against and away from me; there's always a loud version of the same answer.

The intensity of a wavelength, the dread of punishment, all things from pink to plum; this is what we are forced to work with. It isn't so much what you have or haven't thought of, as it is.

As it is

As it is

As it is.

Hands Without Fingers on a Clock Without Time

6.

On your first encounter with the Atlantic Ocean, we
mistook a jellyfish for a plastic bag. Our puzzling
new friend made me proud to be drunk; and you
both drank gin, as I held my Long Island.

Foxed

7.

You like these small cafes; the ones with weird lamps, where conversations waltz between weekend plans and kitchen color combinations.

I watch a dog from the cafe window, while waiting for you to come sit down. Sometimes I wonder if I would be the pet or the owner; this is one of those times.

He looks at me, and starts lapping up some water; you sip your tea, aha!

You start growling about last Friday, so I ask about your kitchen.

You're face turns red; I thought it was blue.

Pinocchio's Pitbulls

8.

Set sail on a Friday.
Bring bananas and a 6-pegged ladder.
Say hello to Davy Jones for me.

Permanent Midnight

9.

Companionship mathematics.
Standing up, walking out from my living room, I
name you Subtraction.
Towards this moment, your footsteps wink at
positivity from behind;
boredom, ampersand, necessity
and I'm thinking of a number, while sitting and alone
and I'm counting breathes and blinks and 4 gives me
a headache; stand up and walk out from my living
room.
What if I had showed you this poem, would that
impress you?
Well-built dogs draw attention because of substance,
and I revised this line about punctuation because I'm
afraid that it wouldn't have been perfect.
And I should have deleted this too, but I wanted you
to come back in.

No Ands Ifs and Ors But Sometimes Whys

10.

The weight of letting in the morning light casts
balance between a sense of floating between the
clouds of dreaming; falling asleep to the sound of
wind instruments, and waking up to lemonade.
My morning is a house, building a prison around my
bed and I can't pay bail or rent or attention to the
radio while my alarm is going off. I am a dark
knight in flat black armor; my sheets are a bed-skirt,
colored school-girl plaid.
The act of dressing my vessel has progressed from a
chore to an elementary-level dance, named Sadie.
My idea of infinity gains splendor in this cell. Dogs
walk by backwards on rewind, and air bubbles are a
life-saving breath underwater; I love silence, infinite
black and a fury of nothingness.
I have everything to gain, while nothing seems
worth it.

Slippery Uphill Slide

11.

The secrets were always kept from us, veiled but of a
whisper. We heard the voice of an unknown saint, and
while starved into illness, we reached for a taste; we
lied. Seven-courses sat above our plates.
I am afraid of your guillotine, and this is the new
majority. We cannot afford the luxuries and secrets,
that the wealthy have discovered. For the lamp,
whose oil burns by the hand of my family, only in
order to service the eyes of our owners, will never
shine bright enough for us to catch a soft glimpse.
Trivial is the square root of Rome's Colosseum, but
as a single succulent seed of what sits beneath our
caps, we have an endless and bittersweet longing for
the knowledge, too rich for thinning red blood.
Our petulance forces the observance of an uprising.
Cheap boots don't have straps, Asshole.

A Vulgar Mouth, Thrice the Wiser

12.

A study was published recently, claiming that a
plant had proven it's own ability of thought.
However, it could not speak or laugh and it could
not properly use a functioning pen; some claimed to
have witnessed a falling tear, while a member of the
crowd began eating an house salad.
Left to it's own devices though, the plant, propped
up on a wooden shelf, released it's own statement on
the topic of thought and the ability to think; it
simply said nothing.

Newtonian

13.

Of these eyes is the lost and found, bound to the metronomic movement of another Earth.

Wink

P

14.

Regret is being alone, practicing your roundhouse
kick.
5am there is 5pm here, and you take cereal for
dinner.
Anxiety is thinking about the Heimlich maneuver.
Satisfaction snores in its sleep, while Craving tries
to write this poem.
Wearing flannel is a nice disguise for creativity.
I burned all of your things to cook this venison.
Honestly, I got up and left a while ago.

Flannel is a Bad Word

15.

On a three-legged chair, before and after an exit sign,
a young cat eats her lunch. There is a small table
before her; clear glass and unfinished wood. Her face
reflects an image of necessity behind the plate, and
she doesn't know if this dish has a name; never will.
Her name is ironic. She starts to sing a song in her
head; one that she had never heard before, but will
never hear the ending of.
A dog walks by;
Newfoundland.

ADHD

16.

She wore an Horus lock and wanted to be a poet.
The only literary works that she had ever enjoyed
reading were old love-letters that she found in her
best-friends attic.
She said that people who read the most, of only the
well-known authors, have nothing original left to
work with. She wanted to learn how to speak
Spanish, not how to read Neruda's Crepusculario. It
took her entire life to find love as wholly
unattainable.

American Typewriter

17.

Our landlord was an uncomfortable, awkward man; like bathroom stalls void of hinged doors. He often gave off the idea of something that you weren't really supposed to be looking at; whatever lies beneath the epidermal layer.

There's nothing wrong with an antisocial personality, but there's a difference between bespectacled shyness and a skittish man who never blinks. We all assumed that his history was littered with memories never too soon forgotten. I mean, he never insisted otherwise; he never insisted much of anything. My landlord reminds me of a story where a child is born on time, but the planets are no longer aligned; not a disappointment, not anything, really.

As luck would have it, our landlord never won the

lottery. If low-stakes gambling were a sport, he wouldn't medal in any division; perhaps he'd be disqualified or quit, like the time he quit on sobriety. The one and only remarkable and breath-taking moment that our landlord would ever be a part of, was jumping from the apex of the eighty-third tallest building in the world.

Splat!

The New York Times Building

18.

Is abstract thought not a redundancy?

I Stood in a Corner and Wondered Why I Keep Thinking of This Though When I'm Forced to Think of Anything in the Entire Universe

19.

A door opened, and out fell a steel revolver. It was cold outside, single-digit Fahrenheit, but the grip of the gun was warm; a stress inducing decision was just made. It was facing down, South, not upwards and on its side of course.

Impatience says to grab, while Spring suggests otherwise. Summertime is nice; who would waste such a season like this?

The Beaumont-Adams revolver was snatched up quickly, and one small silver bullet was liberated from its black barrel.

For the sake of Christ or a Queen, the shot hit its mark; flesh-splitting prettiness.

Shaking with a sudden feeling of foolishness, I fell to the floor, no longer to enjoy conversation with a friend. My face felt particularly brisk at that moment.

How refreshing.

Great Britain, 1859

20.

My glass smiles back at me.
Maybe my head is a big teapot now.
Thirteen thousand of anything is enough to make you
think; something about mass and telescopes and a
long long long long long long long long long long
long long time.
When I shoot stares towards my glass cup, he says
something about where I found him and I look away,
towards everything else.
What was he looking at?
I'm a quiet person today; I had trouble answering
each question thrown my way and nothing.
Nothing
   Nothing
      Nothing
         Nothing
            Nothing
               Nothing
                  Nothing.

The Importance of Nothing

21.

He helped her to her feet, from her back to her
knees. They would spend a lot of time falling in
love.
I can't hear you down there.
Come upstairs to bed.

Timber

22.

On an overcast day in April, a woman lit candles
while trumpets played, and put on her favorite dress.
She had spent 6 years studying the art of asking, and
twice that on secretly clinging to a pill that would
ensue her handsome death. Today was the perfect
day.

She thought about the pale-red blush of Japanese
blossoms and beauty on a cellular level, and when the
last strand of her midnight-blue hair was in just the
right place, she realized that the pill was gone. The
night never answered; like plastic Cherry trees mid-
October.

From that night, her life felt fruitless; abortive. The
seasons developed in monochrome, graceless and
repelling.

She decided to have a child.

Thalia

23.

(As the sun sets, a choir's song is heard)
The effect of my sword
nuanced by his audience
Everyone left that night,
by not the slightest movement.

Poeticism

24.

I am bound by doubt and hunger and sex; so many
things, like roots beneath me.

Drive-by Asphyxiation / Death by Seatbelt

25.

Not quite 10:00 AM, turn out of bed and already
with shoes on, walk outside to a Ford Taurus, fuck
around with a series of keys and scoot along.
11 minutes pass as in a line segment that balls up
into something that doesn't feel like eleven of
anything and more like 1 singular motion; from
bedroom ending at a Methadone clinic, like the most
mundane line segment anyone has ever mapped out
and stopped at the end only to say, *time to do
something else.*
Inside, say *hello* to Tara the half-human/half
computer.
You're good to go!
Great. (Okay.)
In the waiting room, there are 5 people, like the

limbs and head of a lonely human entity that represents impatience, or humility, maybe; one or the other, surely. It's not so much a queue, a line where the front is like heaven and the end is perhaps more like hell, but more resembles something circular; the way a glass half-full might look from directly above, if you were god, up there, looking down, maybe this would look like you're cup of breakfast tea. God probably drinks tea in the morning to feel normal but not *too* normal.

Make it to the end (or the beginning) of the line, circle, segment, shape, place, maybe, and get your fix, and leave to come back again tomorrow, one rotation later.

Pessimism and Robotics

26.

My friend Nicholas likes to make up names.

Flag on the Moon

E

27.

I have an 8:30 appointment at the artery clinic, she says in his ear.

My arms are fucked up to hell.

Hell is a place where things go to remain lost and burn. They burn until they can't burn any longer, but someone tells them to keep burning so they do; Ideally, one could spend a full half-hour in hell before someone find's out they're dead.

He's not sure what an artery clinic is exactly, but it wouldn't be so hard to take a shot in the dark (*she takes shots in the dark once in a while too*). Maybe it's where they fix your veins, very early in the morning, or where she says that she's going when she really means to say, "I can barely keep myself from falling over and curling up into a little ball of

dyed black hair and 2 year old moderately expensive
jeans and skin cells and veins and arteries and those
shoes that look like they're meant for a ballet
dancer's feet, and not mine anymore."
She tells him this and they both find the reasoning
behind being purposely lost.
When 8:30 rolls around, she's driving in a car,
alone, confused as to where her car is right now.
When 8:30 rolls around, he's hoping that she found
help and isn't somewhere lost, plunging white or
brown colored drugs into her arteries. *At least hit the
vein right; you never make it to where you want to
be. It's probably best if you'd just give up*

Thirty-Gauge

28.

Playing in the rain, she made her point. Mark your marvelous bodies dead; dead-center.

Within every ear of corn, every grain's stalk, sits the timid face of thousand diamonds, sitting atop of marbled pillars.

Hallelujah!

Like senses running round desire, pebbles fell from beneath the sky; brains lapped in sped-off races, sitting about, she made herself of a seat. As the pinnacle of life's dreamy gait, I lay bloody; medium rare.

Fed by the troth of heretics, her faith, my faith; the same floor of separate structures. We do not exist in the order of one another's pleasure, nor do we seek to swallow.

The circular struggle of an injured prey becomes static as she watches things end.

A Shibboleth's Polysemy

29.

Beneath the water of the Ozarks are nearly 1500 graves.
It would be a long walk to leave flowers at your headstone, and holding my breath for that long, I'd surely make it to see you.

The Big Fishbowl Up in the Sky

30.

I fucked your brown eyes green and now I'm stuck missing them both separately.

Bifocals

31.

She ran out of conversation. Her mouth wasn't
vacant of speech, she just felt it better to subtract
herself. In a storm, animals and humans alike, feel
the need to find shelter. She would leave in order to
let the wind, the rain, and the storm to be whole
again. In every situation, she felt like a cork of a
bottle, preventing wine from flowing free; like
standing in a stream. She was a comb, moving
through a world of black hair.
She bought roundtrip ticket to Japan, a mid-night
flight.
On her plane, she stood up, took both hands, opened
the door, and stepped out into the sky.
It was her entire life, combing through the cold air,
forcing it to part ways in order for her to exist, and
retrieving its place once she had moved on;
everything flashing before her eyes.
Her body entered the pit-black soil, and now, one
with the Earth, where the lambs walk the hills, she
finally made comfortable conversation; the grass,
her grave, said hello.

In Passing, Locomotive

32.

I never write about dreams, which makes this a lie, an
Aporia, or bad fiction; the rule of threes helps deflect
mistrust. In one recurring dream, my father, a man I
have never met, tells me to draw a table. He says
nothing about himself, but because I am dreaming,
somehow I know that he is a student of alcohol or
opium; one of the two, maybe both.
I try once to draw the table, but I wake up only to
realize that I must have seen that table before.
Perhaps the definitions of words of which I have not
yet learned are simply, an improved state of still not
knowing what to say.

Paradox

M

33.

I am two left turns away from learning if god is just
a nickname.
I am risking your life by taking a picture of my
speedometer.
Let's spend our sight on facelifts, and boast about
our tight-lipped lives. We could be expensive sex-
workers who lost an interest in reading because of
middle-school teachers. Let's kill those middle-
school teachers. We could be happy and thrust
marbles into our cheeks to develop dimples. Let's
smile our way back and forth from insanity, lose our
marbles, and die of syphilis. We could look pretty in
our powdered wigs while we plummet off this cliff.
Let's find god and call her Dickbreath. We could
make a family.

Big Cats Shouldn't Hunt Alone

34.

I spent twenty-five years between green mountains and riots, where ecstasy and fragility marry one another. Far ahead is bearded gray, and far behind is wide-eyed youth. All the while, the moon was hidden from my sight; once too dark, and now to bright. Twenty-five years, I am the musical sound of flight. I am the rhythmic paw of an animal in search of a meal. I am a blue-eyed nymph, buttoning up beneath the rain. I want nothing more than up and out; away from everyday mediocracy, the outside from in-between.

Goodbye green riots, and heavenly hills. Bury us in roses with the scent of a soft perfume. Lead us away from the law, the constant daylight and the unbreakable stride of unquenched thirst. I am many things that die; a kitten, the lawn, and sex-workers. I hope there's candy where we're going.

Nursing Homes

35.

I want a computer that produces tears.
I am the reason for clothing, and fire alarms and
kneepads.
I am more of nothing than I am a lamp to help things
see at night; or unnecessary sunglasses.
I believe in making this computer.

Synchronized Prayer

36.

A pool of smoke follows an automobile, in motion towards the freeway. Careening through one lane and another, a man behind the wheel presses and raises his foot against a pedal.
A smell of burning nature dissipates into the stratosphere, dancing between points A and B.
Two men, perhaps felons whom wish to vote, lift and lower their jaws, while pushing slightly closer to an entrance ramp.
They are unaware of everything except for what is forward.

Charger

37.

Our sleep-cycles mimic a sun at the mercy of the elements.
Why would we choose to display our failures in creativity, and hoist the weight of disappointment above our soft and fragile skulls? For one, my words kick up fallibility, just like everyone else.

Fix This Later For Even Later On

38.

At some point, a man in pursuit or retreat of love,
packed his bags and joined the rat race. While trading
cattails for Chinatowns, and sand-dollars for Wall
Streets, he opted out; and like a high-contrast photo
of February snow blanketing the steep angles of an
uptown duplex, the divorce was a clean break.
Each line between vegetarianism and shaving and
paintings of owls began to soften; a sfumato.
He let go of everything; but, it wasn't so much
liberation as it was surrendering, in defeat of punk
rock and tattoos and everything else a person can
love.
I wonder how men like this feel when looking at the
Mona Lisa or listening to Franz Liszt; the sort of hell,
born in a moment of regret and pantomnesia.
Big cities are where you go to learn how to be
sincerely afraid and alone, covered in rats or other
lonely people.

Stendhal Syndrome

39.

Stare upon my reflection. See his shadow, and make him talk. We laugh, pointing towards rain, while the tapping beyond my window urges us to come out and play.

Meanwhile, a father walks in synchronicity with his third wife; point and laugh, point and laugh.

They walk buy a lonely tree. I watch with my reflection and his shadow. The sound of crows has evaporated, but it's loud from the noise my window and the rain's newfound friendship makes.

Something disappears while we weren't looking, and the man ejaculates beneath his black pants; disgusting and silent. The world's speech changes. The raindrops race down his wives' faces, as my window opens and we all listen for the cacophony of crows.

In me, sings a song of reflections, laughter and shadows. My shrink calls this boredom, but the crows call it crying.

Semantics

40.

Reality opens up the door, somehow screaming with non-chalance. A dream, that one about the horse and the man robbing a bank, has just left you; it's over, and you're awake.

This is regularity. I am as impermanent as a dream is in any revolving vision. You aren't a man robbing a bank, nor are you the horse. You're a symbol of normality while we're awake, and I'm falling back to sleep.

When we get back, I need to eat some breakfast; I'm starting to miss that horse.

Deimos & Phobos

41.

I met a girl who was plagued by nightmares. She was talented, and her source of light came from watching old films; she had dreams of directing her own cinematic masterpiece.

One afternoon, she built up the confidence to phone a producer in Minnesota. She told him of her vision, in which an elephant was hanged by a group of men for quitting it's job at their circus. She described reaching without hands towards tomorrow, struggling slowly as the loss of breath drowns out her cries for help, the elephant's death marks the picture's dour ending.

Not nearly as fun as fishing; they both reflected on sport fishing for more than a second.

Fish don't make noise when they go; some can survive weeks out of water, while an elephant takes hours to finally let go.

She spent her entire life piecing the story together, but her budget was never enough to produce that last scene.

Untitled

42.

My boss once told me, that it's not a party until you
do something that scares you. I had heard the saying
said differently before, but not from my boss and not
in English; not even while awake if I remember
correctly.
It's not a party if you remember it.
It's not a party until someone dies.
It's simply not a party.

Bloomington

43.

You are an anagama.
Behind your face hangs a red mask with silver eyes
and a leering lascivious mouth. Your lips and
tongue excrete frightening sorrowful anger, while
you spit fire upon our bodies and give us life and
death and disabilities.
Your tears turn to ash and are lifted away with an
implication, that when it's your time, you might
collapse in on yourself like a dying star.
Even when you're queen, you're still not the King;
and that's always been reasonable cause for
implosion.

Hannya

44.

A man from Wales traveled about the Congolese river.

Upon his arrival, he was received with a handful of smiling faces; not open arms, but not cold shoulders. It was warm inside and out. His thoughts paced between conditioned air, and leftovers.

He had come to catch a trophy catfish, one to put on a wall in some basement back home, where people lose their appetite when focusing too closely on things. He was born rich, with a wealth that he could carelessly misplace after drinking a glut of Cab Sauv.

A young woman came up to him, laughed, and began talking towards the side of his face. He paid her vocal bijou no attention; a form of currency in which he was short. The scarcity of his heed directed the girl towards anything else, and the man stood alone, looking for a fish.

White Jade

S

45.

If enough people stand in a line, I'll be one of them.
It's deductive reasoning or Black Friday, you do the
math.

Statistics of the Express Lane

46.

I walked down along the river's road, and passed a
glaring and youthful vessel. It's dress had yet to
distinguish a moment of labor from recreation.
Streaming from pebble-like shoulders, to where shins
met skipping-stone heels, clothing remained more of
a practice than a concept.
The sound of small birds, tossing between pine trees,
echoed against the Mississippi faucet. Her ideas
scurry out of sight, putting distance between ears and
things that produce noise; the color Squirrel.
Behind the brightness, stood the omnipresence of
maternity.
"Mother looks of a triangle", thought the vessel's
skipper.
I shot an attempt to draw parallels, between her and

the sky, out of the air.

Clouds caught my eye; something about a butterfly,
a net and metamorphosis.

I'm alone often enough to announce something
brief, in passing of the bug.

She told me that I am tall, if you were wondering.

Ladybird

47.

He complicated the cuteness of our puppy; we had to put him down.

Essence

48.

She hated the idea of becoming a vegetarian; it
could have been the practice of pulling carrots from
the ground that had kept her away.
I quite like my living room today, she thought.
She thought herself to death yesterday.

Adobe

49.

Silence

50.

We cry for families, cursed of the fallen. We pray
through hands with the markings of stigmata. It's as if
evaporated tears have demonstrated your loved one's
whereabouts; an unsaturated soul, once dripping with
life, now floats above us, rising through the slouch of
magnificent heat.
Send signal to the stars; we surrender.

Rebellion, November 20

M

51.

My therapist says that I tend to over-analyze things.
I think that she's right...
...I think that we share this tendency.
It makes sense, if you think about the circumstances.
In her office, there is an off-white lamp that helps
me to see things under a new light; the logic behind
this sort of poeticism is decorative and alluring,
while it sits on a small table, next to my chair.
I just can't quite figure out why it came from the
thrift store;
so I keep coming back.

Yiskah

52.

Picasso's Blue Period could have been a portrayal of
Christ's crucifixion; and when he fucked Dora Maar,
he was resurrected, put down his aquamarine brush,
and reclaimed an interest in pretty poetic pictures.
He died for the prostitutes and the beggars by slaving
over mediocre Zinfandel-affected paintings, in order
to be reborn and confidently sashay towards fresh
polychromatic success; never to remember that ugly
tomb in Jerusalem, or Paris, or Spain somewhere; no
one can say with real certainty.
The only difference is that Maar was infertile, and
Mary would give a virginal birth; semantics, really.

Songbird/Parade

53.

With a whirl, he tailed the prey, his own version of
cat and mouse.

While miming his way down a collection of gray
slate on his barstool legs, he lost his balance and the
fall was punctuated with his head, his mouth, Canine
teeth. My god, hauled out to the emergency room
again and again.

Sitting semi-attentive and fully submerged in an
alcoholic's routine, he asked the assistant, *what time
is it?*

Without a word, she clocked out, walked to a bar,
and pushed over the first stool she saw and the man
fell to a loss of blood.

Adirondack

54.

Katya turns on the radio with her killing hand.

Sedate

55.

Mute by monotony, we paint our faces, cursed in the name of revival.

Your voice was small and hard to hear; low-heat, the whisper of a skillet.

I stare to your statements, fixed upon your blood-red lips. You are pretty.

We sat outside; you, and I, our voices and a clementine.

Harry Houdini

56.

We were all stuck to your pale leaves. A pair of
wandering eyes were sent to the heavens, a statement
of malice and an act of rebellion. The eyes were lost;
loss, loss and more of the same. What is before us
becomes forgotten; like wine in a pan, lifting away an
image, once burned into our polytetrafluoroethylene
eyes.
You are impenetrable. You will once be remembered.
To wake and dress, to wake without; clothed or not,
either way transparent.
What was set in stone, now looms from above, and
we watch you; moving.
Our curiosity was fed by a perpetual hunger, and your
pale leaves, doused in rain, no longer fill our
incessant appetite.

Past-Tense: Lusted

S

57.

You and I trade thoughts, but we're bargaining.
Six of one, half-dozen of the other; we each come
out with an eye for an eye and people love to say
these things over and again. But, whenever we wax
philosophical, the momentum in which you bear is
stale, and run-down conversations always seem to
intercept our masterpiece.
I get the impression that spending our time on apples
or soap and new books could be worthwhile, since I
could be underneath the ground in disrepair making
the same paycheck that I do now.

Quid Pro Quo

58.

By quiet alleys, shrugging with shadows, your mouth
becomes a marvelous flower. At this moment, I am a
servant, and this is your new house; it's a lean dark
dwelling.

Confused, my momentary Cleopatra ponders suicide
and a reason to stay. I suggest a peaceful collision,
not of death and pain, but reddish and physically
willing.

Angled eyebrows, I lie, lying between breasts.

With a blush, your new house becomes a city, and the
alley almost seems clean.

Chimneysweep

59.

Without someone to call hon or dear, I should hold a
stick of dynamite between my jaws and try to
annunciate the consonants of my sayonara.
Beneath my paws, live my soon-to-be pals, and
while I'm out looking for my little muffin, I'll want
to complement the place that they call home, just in
case; just in case I get caught in a motel, and my
lover leaves me to stay at friend's for a while.
Maybe post-bang living wouldn't be all that bad.
Maybe I can't list the justifications for excusing my
head from its shoulders, but I can recite my darling's
name in the same breath as "goodbye".

Jumping to Conclusions/Sometimes Y

60.

Hemmingway once wrote the words:
For sale: baby shoes, never used.
Something along those lines, at least.
He did so on a napkin.
When Ernest was seventeen, William R. Kane wrote:
Little Shoes, Never Worn
At age seventeen, I read Bukowski.
And I don't much care for Hemmingway.
I don't much care for babies or shoes or things along
those lines,
But I do wonder who will be remembered;
The baby or the shoes.

Eliot & Tarantino

61.

Per apathy's aim, may thee ne'er exist forevermore.
Amen

Prex Acedia

62.

...and Judas blew out the lights to spill the salt.

The End

A well-deserved thank you goes out to:

you

my friend and editor, Zach Laskaris

cover artist, Deuce 7

publishing company, Blurb

JES & JES

PT

Kranelegs, because I want your name in a book

my therapist

STRIFE, R.I.P.

Self-Evident

NPR

Top Ramen & Maruchan

my best friend, Lucy Lucifer

Nick D.

Jesse D.

the humans who mistakenly slept next to me

the humans who didn't

the methadone clinic in downtown St. Paul, MN

Ellen C.

a source of sad things, Kelsey L.

a source of happy things, Andy A.

Death Note

& B.

EUPHEMISMS was written by Kevin Stendahl, in
Saint Paul, Minnesota. The collection of poems and
short stories was written between 2015-2016, and
was later compiled for print. During this time, he
worked through a severe drug-addiction and the
deaths of several close friends and family members;
these events are considered to be the key influences
during the creative process of EUPHEMISMS,
along with an overall taste for irony and course
unfiltered humor.

After a series of heroin overdoses and a nearly fatal
car accident, he made the decision to realign his life,
and focus on the release of a book. The book was to
be titled EUPHEMISMS, and was released in 2017.

CPSIA information can be obtained
at www.ICGtesting.com
Printed in the USA
LVHW090918080820
662689LV00003B/785